EDGE BOOKS™

THE TECH BEHIND
ELECTRIC
CARS

by Matt Chandler

CAPSTONE PRESS
a capstone imprint

Edge Books are published by Capstone Press,
1710 Roe Crest Drive, North Mankato, Minnesota 56003
www.capstonepub.com

Library of Congress Cataloging-in-Publication Data
Names: Chandler, Matt, author.
Title: The tech behind electric cars / by Matt Chandler.
Description: First edition. | North Mankato, Minnesota : Capstone Press,
    [2020] | Series: Edge books. Tech on wheels. | Audience: Age 8-14. |
    Audience: Grades 7 to 8.
Identifiers: LCCN 2018060563|
ISBN 9781543573077 (hardcover) | ISBN 9781543573114 (ebook pdf)
Subjects: LCSH: Electric automobiles—Juvenile literature.
Classification: LCC TL220 .C4525 2020 | DDC 629.22/93—dc23
LC record available at https://lccn.loc.gov/2018060563

Editorial Credits
Carrie Braulick Sheely, editor; Jennifer Bergstrom, designer; Eric Gohl, media researcher;
Katy LaVigne, production specialist

Photo Credits
AP Photo: Duane Burleson, 14, Koji Sasahara, 10; iStockphoto: Tramino, 24 (top); Library of
Congress: 7; Newscom: dpa/picture-alliance/Marijan Murat, 19, Reuters/Staff, 26, WENN/
Michael Wright, 23, ZUMA Press/Rodrigo Reyes Marin, 20; Shutterstock: apiguide, 13, Dong
Liu, 29, Grzegorz Czapski, cover, 22, 28, Imagenet, 18, Marco Iacobucci EPP, 16, Massimo
Parisi, 4, metamorworks, 12, 24 (bottom), NosorogUA, 17, Yauhen_D, 8; SuperStock:
Science and Society, 6

Design Elements: Shutterstock

Printed in and bound in the USA.
PA70

TABLE OF CONTENTS

A Nissan Leaf sits in a parking spot reserved for electric vehicles in London, England. The Nissan Leaf is the world's best-selling electric vehicle.

CHAPTER 1

THE HUGE COMEBACK OF ELECTRIC CARS

Imagine the year is 2040. You back out of your driveway and stomp down on the gas pedal. As you zip down the road, you are surrounded by cars. But the streets are quiet. You pull into a charging station for electric cars. In just 15 minutes your car is fully charged, and you head back out on the highway.

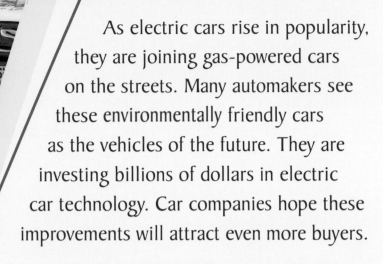

As electric cars rise in popularity, they are joining gas-powered cars on the streets. Many automakers see these environmentally friendly cars as the vehicles of the future. They are investing billions of dollars in electric car technology. Car companies hope these improvements will attract even more buyers.

Early Rise of Electric Cars

Electric cars may seem new, but they are actually older than gas-powered cars. The earliest models of the 1830s didn't look like any of today's cars. An electric car was not much more than a wooden platform with bench seats and four wheels. With batteries that weren't rechargeable, these vehicles weren't very useful.

FACT
In 2018, electric car sales in the U.S. grew by more than 80 percent from 2017 sales.

environment—the air, water, trees, and other natural surroundings

French scientist Gaston Planté created the world's first rechargeable battery in 1859. His invention paved the way for better electric vehicles.

British inventor Thomas Parker built the first practical electric car in 1884. Three years later, American William Morrison built the first successful electric car in the United States. Electric cars quickly became popular in New York and other large U.S. cities. But this popularity didn't last.

Putting on the Brakes

In 1908, Ford Motor Company built its first Model Ts. In 1912, most Model Ts cost between $600 and $900. An electric car cost more than $1,700. In 1913, Ford began using an assembly line to make Model Ts, which lowered the price further. Driven by cost, most people chose to buy Ford's gas-powered cars.

Gaston Planté's rechargeable battery

Andrew Riker drives his electric car across the finish line to win a car race on Long Island, New York, in 1900. It was the only electric vehicle in the race.

Yet as electric cars faded into the background, scientists and inventors kept working on electric vehicle technology. They spent years improving it to make electric cars competitive with gas-powered vehicles.

assembly line—an arrangement of machines, equipment, and workers in which work passes from operation to operation in direct line until the product is assembled

practical—fit for use

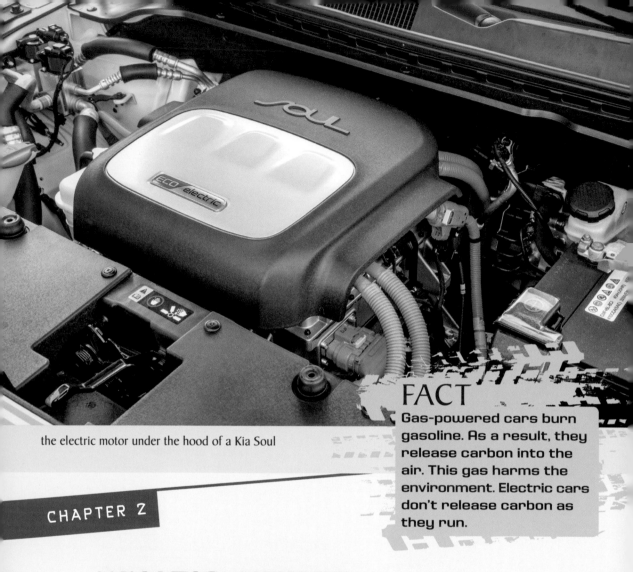

the electric motor under the hood of a Kia Soul

CHAPTER 2

WHAT'S UNDER THE HOOD?

The work that designers put into electric cars has paid off today. Cutting-edge tech is packed into an electric car, especially in the engine and battery. These parts are key to how an electric car works.

Electric Car Motors

If you pop open the hood of an electric car, you'll see the motor is very different from a gas-powered engine. If you touch the engine of a gas-powered car after a drive home, you'll burn your hand. Gas engines operate by creating massive friction between interlocking metal parts in the engine connected to a driveshaft. The heat created by this friction is wasted energy. It wears down the engine and leads to breakdowns.

An electric car has an induction motor. Electric induction motors work by using electromagnets to create magnetic fields. Magnetic fields make a part called a rotor spin. These motors produce almost no heat at all, making them more efficient.

Electric car motors need fewer parts than gas-powered engines. Their simple design also makes them very efficient. With fewer parts, breakdowns are less frequent.

driveshaft—the parts of a vehicle that transfer power to the wheels

efficient—the quality of not wasting time or energy

electromagnet—a magnet that is temporarily magnetized by an electric current

friction—a force created when two objects rub together

Better Batteries

The battery supplies electricity to make an electric car run. For this reason, car companies have put a lot of focus on batteries in recent years. Gas-powered cars use lead-acid batteries that cost as little as $100. Electric cars use lithium-ion battery packs that cost thousands of dollars.

A Nissan employee holds a module of an electric car's battery pack. The module is made up of battery cells that are enclosed in a metal case. Modules are put together in a pack on the bottom of the car.

In 2010, an electric car battery cost about $1,000 per kilowatt-hour (kWh). Automakers had to find ways to be more efficient in their battery development to bring the cost down. Tesla has been a leader in battery technology. By 2019, Tesla's Model 3 had come with a battery pack priced at about $150 per kilowatt-hour. Experts believe Tesla may soon be able to get the price to $100 kWh.

PROMISING BATTERY TECH

Lithium-ion batteries are very lightweight. But designers are always working to make them lighter. The less a car weighs, the longer it can run on a single electric charge. Developers are testing a new tech for batteries using a carbon-based material called graphene. It makes the batteries lighter. It also allows them to be charged five times faster than traditional batteries. Graphene batteries can allow electric cars to travel 500 miles (805 kilometers) on a single charge!

electricity—the flow or stream of charged particles, such as electrons

kilowatt-hour—a unit of work or energy equal to that expended by one kilowatt in one hour

Controllers Are Key

Once the battery is charged, the power is ready for the car to use. But it needs to get to the engine. That's where the controller comes in. When the driver presses the gas pedal, a signal goes to a pair of devices called potentiometers. They send a signal to the controller to tell it how much electricity to send to the engine. The harder the driver presses the gas, the more electricity the controller sends to the engine.

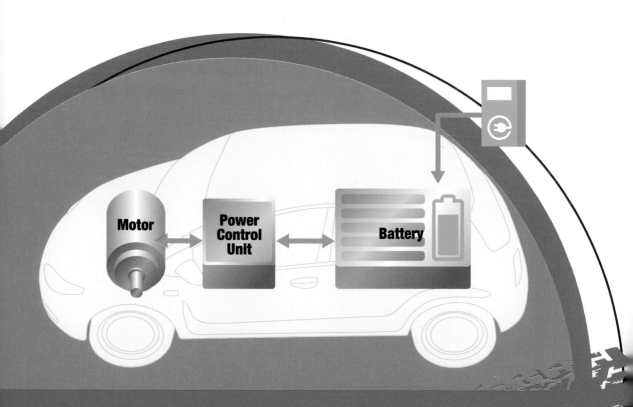

Motor

Power Control Unit

Battery

The battery, motor, and control unit work together so an electric car can operate.

HYBRID CARS: THE BEST OF BOTH WORLDS

Hybrid cars combine electric power and gasoline power in one car. They use both a small gas engine and a small electric motor. The electric engine powers the car at low speeds. The gas engine takes over at higher speeds.

Toyota is a top manufacturer of hybrid cars. In 1997, the Prius became the first modern hybrid car sold to the public. In 2017, six of the top 10 best-selling hybrids were Toyotas.

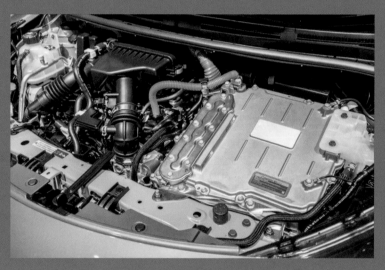

the gas motor (left) and the electric motor (right) of a hybrid car

Did you ever wonder why electric cars are so quiet compared to gas-powered vehicles? It is the technology found in the controller. It pulses the power from the batteries to the engine at more than 15,000 cycles per second. At that speed, the noise can't be picked up by the human ear!

Car manufacturers put electric batteries through tests to be sure they work properly.

CHAPTER 3

SAFETY AND EFFICIENCY

Safety and efficiency are big priorities for car buyers. Car companies consider both when making electric cars. They are always searching for ways to make electric cars safer and even more efficient.

A Scary Video

In 2018, Hollywood actress Mary McCormack posted a scary video to social media. It showed her husband's Tesla Model S on fire. The fire appeared to start in the battery pack. The video spread to many others on social media and raised concerns about the safety of electric cars.

Lithium-ion batteries contain a flammable liquid called electrolyte. If the battery cells short-circuit, they can overheat. When this happens, a chemical reaction can occur that causes the cells to catch fire. This process is called thermal runaway. Although electric battery fires are rare, Tesla and other manufacturers have tech to help prevent them. Thermal cooling systems help keep the cells from overheating. Tesla came up with its own idea for a new energy storage system. It would keep one damaged battery cell from affecting other cells.

electrolyte—a substance that is capable of conducting an electric current when melted or dissolved in water

short-circuit—a type of interruption in the regular flow of electricity through a circuit; short circuits can cause overheating or circuit damage

Extra Efficiency

Electric cars are already very efficient. But that doesn't mean designers stop trying to improve.

Regenerative braking is one feature that adds to an electric car's efficiency. When the brakes are applied in a gas-powered car, the brake pads and rotors grind and wear down. With regenerative braking, when a driver steps on the brake pedal, the vehicle's engine starts spinning in reverse. This slows the car without the use of heat-creating friction. Electric cars still have friction brakes as a backup. But automatic braking creates less wear and tear on the brakes. They last much longer.

FACT

Formula E electric race cars use regenerative braking. A new brake-by-wire system for the 2018–2019 season is designed to give drivers better control.

Many parts of an electric car connect with the wheels. Some of these parts move the car or are part of the braking system. Others help provide a smoother ride.

There is another advantage of regenerative braking. The faster a car is moving, the more kinetic energy it creates. As the electric car slows down, this energy is captured. It is then changed, or converted, back to chemical energy. This energy is sent back to the batteries. That means that as it drives, an electric car is recharging its batteries!

kinetic energy—the energy of a moving object

Electric cars do have some disadvantages compared to gas-powered cars. They take a long time to recharge and have less range than gas-powered cars do. Filling a gas tank of a car takes just a few minutes and can last for 300 to 400 miles (483 to 644 km). In comparison, most electric cars take at least eight hours to recharge with a standard charger that plugs into a wall outlet. Once charged, an electric car won't get near the range of a gas-powered vehicle. For example, the Nissan Leaf has a range of 150 miles (241 km).

Many electric cars have charging ports on the side of the vehicle behind the doors.

Porsche produces its Taycan at its plant in Stuttgart, Germany.

Electric car designers are trying to improve the time it takes electric cars to recharge. Porsche is leading the way. The company expects the battery in its Taycan sports car to recharge to 80 percent in just 15 minutes.

range—the maximum distance a vehicle or craft can travel without refueling or recharging

The Nissan Formula E race car (left) and the Leaf Nismo RC (right) were at the Tokyo Auto Salon show in 2019.

CHAPTER 4

ALL ABOUT PERFORMANCE

Electric cars are all about efficiency. But does this awesome efficiency mean less performance compared to gas-powered cars? This is a question some car buyers have. Electric car designers are wasting no time in making sure buyers get the best performance possible.

The Power of Two Motors

Some electric car designers are focused on increasing power. One way to give cars a horsepower boost is to use two motors. In 2018, Nissan released a new version of its electric race car, the Leaf Nismo RC. Its two motors produce 322 horsepower. That is more than double the power of the street version of the Nissan Leaf. The Nismo RC goes from 0 to 60 miles (97 km) per hour in 3.4 seconds.

The two-engine electric Tesla S P100D accelerates even faster than the LEAF Nismo RC. It reaches 60 miles (97 km) per hour in 2.5 seconds! This car has one motor controlling the front wheels and the other one controlling the rear. This design helps the car handle better than a one-motor electric car too.

accelerate—to increase the speed of a moving object

horsepower—a unit for measuring an engine's power

Need for Speed

The fast acceleration speeds of the Leaf Nismo RC and the Tesla S P100D are amazing. These speeds come easier for an electric car than they would for a gas-powered car. A gas-powered car runs on a transmission that shifts gears as the car speeds up. An electric car doesn't need a transmission that shifts gears, so it gains speed faster. Imagine a gas-powered car and an electric car are at a stop sign. As the light turns green, the electric car would speed right by the other car!

A Tesla S P100D was on display at the Paris Motor Show in 2018.

But although they accelerate quickly, electric cars have lower top speeds than most gas-powered cars. Tesla limits its P90Ds and P100Ds to top speeds of 155 miles (249 km) per hour. They are two of the fastest electric cars available today. Dozens of high-performance production gas-powered cars can top 200 miles (322 km) per hour. For example, the 2019 Dodge Challenger SRT Hellcat Redeye maxes out at 203 miles (327 km) per hour.

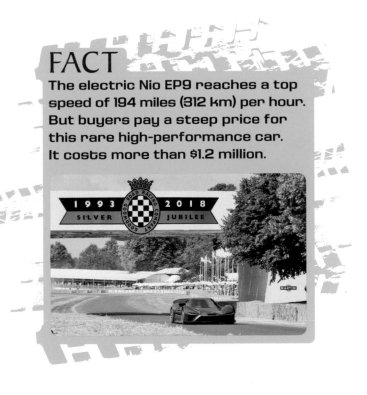

FACT
The electric Nio EP9 reaches a top speed of 194 miles (312 km) per hour. But buyers pay a steep price for this rare high-performance car. It costs more than $1.2 million.

production—describes a vehicle produced for mass-market sale

A Toyota Mirai hydrogen-powered car refuels at a station in Warsaw, Poland.

CHAPTER 5

DRIVING INTO THE FUTURE

The popularity of electric cars is rising quickly. Yet most people still drive gas-powered vehicles. In 2017, more than 86 million cars were purchased worldwide. Only about 1 million of them were electric cars. In the future, car manufacturers will need to make some changes to draw more people to electric vehicles.

Are Fuel Cells the Future?

Limited driving ranges are holding back electric car sales. For electric cars to become mainstream, technology has to address this issue. Hydrogen-powered electric cars could be widely available within the next 10 years. Unlike regular electric cars, they have a fuel tank that is filled with hydrogen. A block of fuel cells is in front of the tank. The hydrogen is mixed with oxygen and fed through the fuel cells to produce electricity.

Hydrogen-powered cars have two main advantages over battery-powered cars. Many electric cars have a range of less than 150 miles (240 km). A hydrogen-powered car has a range similar to a gas vehicle of up to about 400 miles (640 km) per fill-up. When it is time to fill up, hydrogen is pumped like gasoline. Refilling takes five to 10 minutes. However, in 2018, there were only 39 hydrogen refueling stations in the United States. Most of them are in California. It will take a major investment in a refueling network to make hydrogen cars a real option.

hydrogen—a colorless gas that is lighter than air and burns easily

Solid-State Battery Tech

Some carmakers are researching solid-state battery technology to increase electric car ranges. This tech could allow drivers to cruise 1,000 miles (1,609 km) on a single charge. Solid-state batteries would use solid electrolytes instead of the liquid that lithium-ion batteries use. They would reduce the risk of battery fires while storing twice as much energy.

A researcher shows a design of a solid-state battery under development in 2017.

Cool Concepts

Many companies are trying to set themselves apart from competitors with unique vehicles. To show off their designs, they create concept cars. Among them is the BMW iX3 Electric. Many electric cars are small or medium-sized cars. The iX3 is an SUV. It comes with some of BMW's most advanced technology.

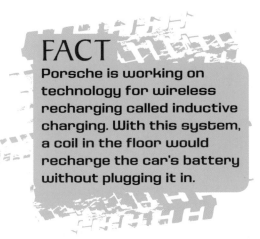

FACT
Porsche is working on technology for wireless recharging called inductive charging. With this system, a coil in the floor would recharge the car's battery without plugging it in.

concept car—a car built to show a new idea; only some concept cars go into production

The iX3 SUV will travel nearly 250 miles (402 km) on a single charge. When the battery does run low, the new BMW will support 150-kilowatt fast charging, giving drivers a nearly full charge in 30 minutes.

The BMW iX3 concept car has a front grille shaped to help reduce the force of air moving against it. With less air resistance, a car can move faster.

NO STEERING WHEEL NEEDED!

Nissan and many other manufacturers are combining the technology of electric cars with self-driving cars. If you jumped into Nissan's IDS self-driving concept car, you'd notice something is missing—the steering wheel! With no driver needed, it is replaced with a tablet. But if drivers do want to drive, they can press a button. Then a dashboard opens, and the wheel appears!

FACT

The electric BMW i3 takes being environmentally friendly to the next level. Some plastics in the interior are made from natural fibers of plants.

Do you like the idea of one day driving an electric car? You may never have to pump gas or get a single oil change. As the technology improves, you may never even have to plug in your electric car. For now, gas-powered cars still rule the roads. But electric cars may be the future of driving!

GLOSSARY

accelerate (ak-SEL-uh-rayt)—to increase the speed of a moving object

assembly line (uh-SEM-blee LYN)—an arrangement of machines, equipment, and workers in which work passes from operation to operation in direct line until the product is assembled

concept car (KAHN-sept KAR)—a car built to show a new idea; only some concept cars go into production

driveshaft (DRYV-shaft)—the parts of a vehicle that transfer power to the wheels

efficient (uh-FI-shuhnt)—the quality of not wasting time or energy

electricity (i-lek-TRI-suh-tee)—the flow or stream of charged particles, such as electrons

electrolyte (i-LEK-truh-lyte)—a substance that is capable of conducting an electric current when melted or dissolved in water

electromagnet (i-lek-troh-MAG-nuht)—a magnet that is temporarily magnetized by an electric current

environment (in-VY-ruhn-muhnt)—the air, water, trees, and other natural surroundings

friction (FRIK-shuhn)—a force created when two objects rub together

horsepower (HORSS-pou-ur)—a unit for measuring an engine's power

hydrogen (HYE-druh-juhn)—a colorless gas that is lighter than air and burns easily

kilowatt-hour (KIL-uh-waht-AU-ur)—a unit of work or energy equal to that expended by one kilowatt in one hour

kinetic energy (ki-NET-ik EN-ur-jee)—the energy of a moving object

practical (PRAK-ti-kuhl)—fit for use

production (pruh-DUHK-shuhn)—describes a vehicle produced for mass-market sale

range (RAYNJ)—the maximum distance a vehicle or craft can travel without refueling or recharging

short-circuit (SHORT SUR-kut)—a type of interruption in the regular flow of electricity through a circuit; short circuits can cause overheating or circuit damage

READ MORE

Diaz, Julio. *Tesla Model S.* Vroom! Hot Cars. Vero Beach, FL: Rourke Educational Media, 2016.

Eschbach, Christina. *Inside Electric Cars.* Inside Technology. Minneapolis: Abdo Pub., 2019.

Graham, Ian. *From Falling Water to Electric Car.* Energy Journeys. Chicago: Heinemann, 2015.

INTERNET SITES

Electric Vehicle Benefits
https://www.energy.gov/eere/electricvehicles/electric-vehicle-benefits

How Do All-Electric Cars Work?
https://afdc.energy.gov/vehicles/how-do-all-electric-cars-work

Timeline: History of the Electric Car
http://www.pbs.org/now/shows/223/electric-car-timeline.html

INDEX